Series 644

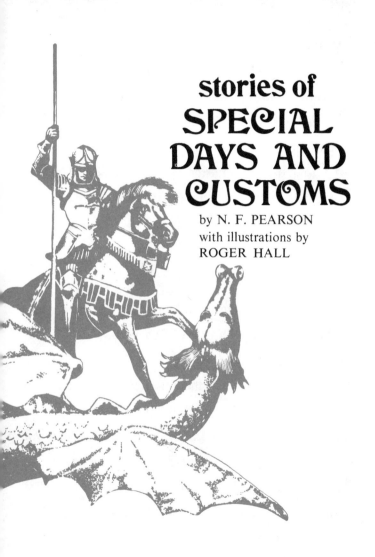

stories of SPECIAL DAYS AND CUSTOMS

by N. F. PEARSON

with illustrations by
ROGER HALL

Publishers: Ladybird Books Ltd . Loughborough
© Ladybird Books Ltd (formerly Wills & Hepworth Ltd) 1972
Printed in England

Anniversaries

We look forward every year to certain days which we know will bring special treats. At Christmas people give presents, send cards and put up decorations, and young children look forward to a visit from Santa Claus. At Easter there are Easter eggs; on Good Friday hot cross buns, and on November 5th, fireworks. These and many other days are anniversaries, for they come 'annually' or 'yearly'. Your birthday comes every year, so that is also an anniversary.

The most important anniversary is Christmas, which includes not only Christmas Day itself, but days like New Year's Day and Boxing Day. So much happens during Christmas that there is a Ladybird book — 'Christmas Customs' — about the Christmas season. After Christmas comes Easter, and this book tells you the reasons why we have eggs at Easter, why people play 'duck-apple' on Halloween Night, why we have fireworks on November 5th, and the reasons for many other annual customs.

A birthday party

0 7214 0308 5

New Year

The first and last days of the year have always been regarded as special days — days when we look back on the year that has gone and look forward to the coming year. Many people make New Year resolutions to lead better lives in the future.

New Year celebrations start on the last day of the old year, New Year's Eve. There is usually plenty to eat and drink. Most people stay up until midnight to see the Old Year out and the New Year in. Some see the New Year in by going to special midnight services at their churches, where bells ring in the New Year. Others go to social gatherings where the New Year is begun by the singing of 'Auld Lang Syne'. This is an ancient Scottish folk song which we might never have had but for the famous poet, Robert Burns. He heard the chorus and probably the first verse, which he wrote down and then added more verses of his own.

Many more people celebrate at home by observing the world-wide folk custom of 'first footing'. This is for a man or a boy to be the first to enter the house after midnight and to wish all inside 'A Happy New Year'.

February 14th: St. Valentine's Day

A Saint Valentine certainly lived in the 3rd century, but so much legend surrounds him that we do not know the true facts about his life. There may even have been two Saint Valentines, both beheaded about the year 270 A.D. for preaching about Jesus.

The only connection between the saint and the practice of giving valentines is that his day, February 14th, was close to the pagan Roman feast of Lupercalia. One of the customs of Lupercalia was for boys to draw girls' names on slips of paper from an urn. This custom was brought to Britain by the Romans. Towards the end of the 5th century Lupercalia was forbidden, but drawing names in this way was so popular that it continued, in spite of some priests who tried to stop it. The custom continued right up to the 18th century.

Valentine verses in praise of a loved one are known to have been written as far back as Shakespeare's time. By 1800, valentine verse cards were being printed. As printing and posting became easier and cheaper, the sending of cards became more popular. Through the centuries, choosing a 'sweetheart' by drawing lots has changed to sending a card — a 'valentine' — to the person one would *like* to choose. The card is sent unsigned so that the person who receives it does not know who the sender is.

February 29th: Leap Day

A solar year is the time it takes our planet to make one circle round the sun. It takes the Earth 365¼ days to do this. It is impossible to have a quarter of a day, so to make the calendar year as near as possible to the solar year, we add an extra day every fourth year. This is added to the end of February, which usually has 28 days, so we then have a February 29th every four years.

However, the actual solar year is 365 days 5 hours 48 minutes 46 seconds. In 384 years the calendar year would be out by 3 days. To right this, no year which ends with two 'noughts' is a Leap Year, unless it can be divided by 400. Our calendar year is correct to less than a day in 20,000 years.

'Leap Year' is so called because after a February 29th, the days of the week jump two week-days ahead of the previous year. If, for example, in an ordinary year, July 7th falls on a Sunday, the next year it will fall on a Monday, unless that next year is a Leap Year, when it will 'leap' over Monday and fall on Tuesday.

There is a custom that in Leap Year a woman may ask a man to marry her. No-one knows how this came about, although there are some old laws which make this legal.

Sosigenes, astronomer of Alexandria, explaining the need for a Leap Year. (46 B.C.)

March 1st: St. David's Day

March 1st is reputed to be the day on which St. David, the patron saint of Wales, died. He is remembered by the wearing of a daffodil. For centuries the leek was regarded as the national emblem. St. David was supposed to have won a great battle and to have ordered his soldiers to wear leeks as distinguishing marks. The confusion over the national emblem may have arisen because the Welsh words for leek and daffodil are almost the same. The daffodil, or Lent lily, probably originated with the lily of France, for Welsh soldiers are thought to have brought it back after taking part in the French battles of Henry V.

Countless legends are told of St. David, but all we can be sure of is that he spent most of his life preaching in Wales during the 6th century. Tradition tells that once, while preaching, a white dove settled on his shoulder and the ground on which he stood rose into a hill.

Another legend tells us that after David was made a bishop, he moved to a remote headland and there built his cathedral city of St. David's. Here he was buried. During the Middle Ages his shrine was an important place of pilgrimage.

St. David preaching

Pancake Tuesday

'Pancake' or 'Shrove' Tuesday is the day before Lent. Lent was once a time of fasting when Christians went without certain foods, to show that they were sorry for the wrongs they had done. The day before, they were 'shriven' in church, which means they confessed their sins and were forgiven. From 'shriving', Shrove Tuesday gets its name.

Food forbidden during Lent was eaten up before Lent began. Careful housewives used their remaining eggs and fats in pancakes, and as pancakes were both tasty and filling it was a good way to 'fill up' before the fast. It is possible that early Christians were following a tradition much older than Christ, for in Ancient Rome at this time of the year, little cakes were made and eaten in worship of Fornax, goddess of ovens.

In Britain, the making of pancakes is all that remains of Shrovetide customs. In some places pancake races are held, when housewives race one another while tossing a pancake in a frying pan. Once, Shrovetide was a time of carnival, fun and mischief. 'Carnival', a word derived from Latin, means 'farewell to flesh', for meat was not allowed in Lent, so everyone ate well beforehand. In many Roman Catholic countries, Shrovetide is carnival time. In parts of France and the United States of America, the carnival is called 'Mardi Gras', which means 'Fat Tuesday'.

Mardi Gras celebrations in New Orleans, U.S.A.

Ash Wednesday

Ash Wednesday is the first day of Lent. Lent lasts until Easter Sunday and is a solemn time when Christians think of the events leading to the Crucifixion. In spring, days get lighter; each day has more light than the previous day, so the Saxons called spring 'lencten time' because the days 'lengthened', and from this we get our word 'Lent'.

The first day of Lent became Ash Wednesday because Lent started with the act of marking a cross, with a finger dipped in ashes, on the foreheads of all who went to church. This custom is still practised in the Roman Catholic Church, and the priests who make the ash mark are carrying out a custom which is a thousand years old.

Ashes are, of course, what is left after a fire, but these ashes are special because they are the ashes of the palms that have been used the previous year on Palm Sunday. The palms are burned and the ashes kept for this day.

The ash marks are a sign of sorrow for the cruel death of Jesus, and they also show that the wearer is sorry for his own sins.

A priest marks a forehead with a cross of ash

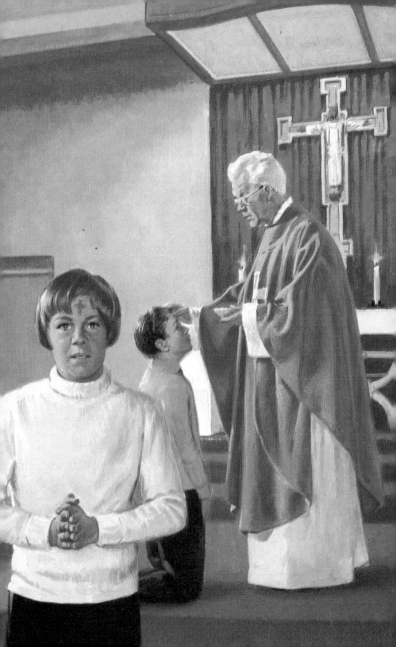

March 17th: St. Patrick's Day

March 17th, St. Patrick's Day, is the most important Irish holiday of the year. The Irish patron saint is remembered by the wearing of the shamrock, for St. Patrick is said to have used the shamrock to explain the Holy Trinity. He said that as the shamrock was one leaf in three parts so God was one God with three parts, Father, Son and Spirit.

Little is known of Patrick's real life, for there are so many legends about him. As a youth he was carried off to Ireland and sold as a slave. He spent six years tending the herds of an Irish chieftain before he escaped to France, where he entered a monastery. Some years later he had a dream about a man called Victorious, who showed Patrick a letter which began, — "The voice of the Irish . . . ." As Patrick repeated these words he heard Irish voices saying, "We pray thee, holy youth, to come and walk again amongst us as before". So Patrick prepared to be a missionary and after many years' preparation returned to Ireland where, after a long life devoted to the Christian mission, he died on 17th March, A.D. 461.

St. Patrick has a dream

April 1st: All Fools Day

Most boys and girls do their best to play tricks on other people during the first morning in April.

'Fooling' at this time of the year can be traced back to remote times, and is to be found in many parts of the world. At the feast of Huli, celebrated at the end of March, Hindus of India send 'fools' on fruitless errands. The Ancient Romans had a similar custom. In France a fool, being 'as stupid as a fish', is called an 'April fish'. The first fools were 'April fish' because they continued to celebrate New Year on April 1st, the old New Year's Day, when the rest of France had changed the day to January 1st. A foolish person is sometimes called a cuckoo. In Scotland the fool is an 'April gowk', which means 'April cuckoo'.

All these customs took place, and still take place, soon after March 21st, the first day of spring.'Fooling' seems one of the ways in which people show the renewed liveliness and joy which accompany the spring season.

An April Fool trick

Mothering Sunday

This is the day on which we say 'thank you' to our mothers who, all the year round, do so much for us. Usually we give them gifts and most often gifts of flowers. Some people give special cakes, called Simnel cakes. These are rich fruit cakes, sometimes thickly covered with almond paste. Cakes like this have been made for over a thousand years.

Mothering Sunday is the fourth Sunday in Lent. It comes at this time of the year because, in pagan times before people were Christians, they worshipped a goddess called Cybele who was known as the great Mother of the Gods. When people no longer believed in many gods and goddesses, they still wanted a day to remember their mothers, and so we have Mothering Sunday.

When Christian people first went to live in the United States of America, they forgot about Mothering Sunday. However, mothers are remembered there — not on Mothering Sunday but on the second Sunday in May, which is called Mother's Day and is a national holiday.

Cybele, mother of the ancient gods

Palm Sunday

"The next day a great body of pilgrims who had come to the festival, hearing that Jesus was on His way to Jerusalem, took palm branches and went out to meet Him, shouting 'Hosanna!'. Jesus found a donkey and mounted it."

In these words, Saint John tells us how Jesus rode into Jerusalem for the last time. We remember this on Palm Sunday.

For more than fifteen hundred years, Roman Catholics have remembered the day by having palm branches blessed and carried in procession before Mass. The palms are brought for this purpose from the Holy Land. When most English people belonged to the Roman Catholic Church, they had palm processions, but as palms do not grow naturally in our country, branches of other trees were used. A great favourite was the lovely catkin-covered willow. Long ago, in some places a wooden statue of Christ mounted on a donkey was pulled through the streets.

Only a few Protestant churches are decorated with palms or willows, although some churches give away crosses of palm. Worship on Palm Sunday will include the singing of that fine hymn, 'Ride on, ride on in majesty'.

Maundy Thursday

It is probable that 'Maundy' comes from the Latin word 'mandatum' which means 'commandment', for on the Thursday before Good Friday, Jesus said, "A new commandment I give unto you, that ye love one another". This was said while the Disciples were eating the Last Supper. Just before they sat down to eat, Jesus showed His love for them by washing their feet. It is these happenings that we remember on Maundy Thursday.

About three hundred years after the death of Jesus, it became the habit of all noblemen, from the Pope to kings and priests, to wash the feet of twelve, or more, poor men. In our country, the reigning king washed the feet of as many poor men as he was years old. After he had done this, he gave them money, food and clothes. From 1661 this money consisted of specially minted, silver coins, called 'Maundy pennies'. In 1754 foot-washing stopped, but Maundy pennies are still given, and the number of money-bags presented is the same as the number of years the king or queen has lived.

Carrying the bags of 'Maundy' money

Good Friday

Good Friday is the day each year when we remember the cruel death of Jesus and how He was nailed to a cross. In the days before motor vehicles, when horses were used to pull carts and carriages, blacksmiths would not shoe horses on Good Friday, or use nails in any other way because of the nails that had hurt Jesus. It seems that Good Friday used to be called God's Friday, which is really a much better name for the day.

One of the ways we remember Good Friday is by eating hot cross buns. Christians like to think that the cross on the bun is in memory of Christ's cross, but buns with crosses were used in the worship of gods and goddesses before Jesus lived. It seems likely that the early Christians gave a new meaning to a very old custom.

You probably know the rhyme 'Hot cross buns! Hot cross buns! One a penny, Two a penny, Hot cross buns!' This is what the bakers used to cry long ago as they went through the streets with their trays of buns on Good Friday morning.

Selling hot cross buns on Good Friday

Easter Sunday

After He was crucified, Jesus was seen to be alive again. This we remember on Easter Sunday. Jesus returning to the world reminded people of new life which returns to trees and plants in spring. As Jesus was crucified in spring, the first Christians remembered Him with many of the customs they had once used at their spring festivals. Eostre was goddess of spring and it is from her festival that we get the name Easter.

This is the day for Easter eggs. The making of chocolate eggs is not a very old custom, but real eggs have been given as spring gifts for thousands of years by people in many parts of the world. Before Jesus was born, specially-coloured eggs were given by the ancient peoples of Persia and Egypt at spring festivals, for eggs look as dead as winter, and yet, like plants in winter, they contain the beginning of new spring life. In several countries today it is still the practice to hard-boil eggs and paint patterns on the shells. The new life in the egg probably reminded Christians of the new life — the resurrection — of Jesus. As eggs were forbidden food in Lent, people were very glad to eat them once more.

Eostre, Goddess of spring

Easter Monday

Holy Week having been a time for sadness and serious thought, on Easter Monday people are ready to enjoy themselves. So on this day sports and games are played in most Christian countries. There are special professional football matches, and keen amateurs often play on this day. These games are just the modern part of a long history of many different, and some strange, games played on Easter Monday.

Egg rolling is still a favourite game. Easter Monday egg rolling, down grassy slopes, is played in many parts of northern Britain. Eggs are also rolled on the lawns of the home of the President of the United States of America.

In England, until this century, there used to be a strange game called 'lifting'. On Easter Monday men carried a flower-decked chair. Each woman they met they lifted three times in it. On Easter Tuesday the women did the same to the men. There is a record of Edward I being 'lifted' by the ladies of the court. The one lifted was expected to pay a small forfeit, but Edward paid a forfeit of fourteen pounds!

April 23rd: St. George's Day

Although not an Englishman, St. George is the patron saint of England, and his red cross on white is part of the British flag. He was an early soldier martyr, of whom we know very little. Probably he was born and buried in Lydda, Israel. He was severely tortured for refusing to give up his faith and died on April 23rd, 303 A.D.

He is remembered most of all for the legend of the dragon. One day he came upon a princess, weeping beside a lake. She told him she was waiting to be devoured by the dragon of the lake, for every day one person had to be sacrificed to it. St. George fought with the monster and killed it.

All over Christendom from early times, St. George was a popular saint, particularly with soldiers. It is said that the crusaders of the eleventh century saw him in a vision and were victorious. From that time his name became a battle-cry of the English armies and his red cross became an English symbol. Edward III founded the Order of the Garter by which the saint is remembered. Members of this ancient order still meet at St. George's Chapel, Windsor, on the saint's day.

St. George and the dragon

May 1st: May Day

In some parts of the country, children still dress up as May Queens, with their retinues of courtiers. Children who do this are continuing a very old custom.

In pre-Christian days, May was the time of the year when spring was celebrated. The Romans honoured Flora, goddess of flowering plants, by gathering flowers to adorn her temple. When they conquered our country and other lands, they brought this custom with them. After they left and Christianity became the main faith, spring was still celebrated with flowers.

Everyone went 'a-maying' in the Middle Ages and Tudor times. They rose at sunrise and collected blossom which was brought back to the towns and villages with much fun and merrymaking. Hawthorn blossom is called 'may', because it is picked at this time. When the town or village was reached, a maypole was set up and gaily decorated with wreaths of flowers and ribbons. After this, the May King and May Queen were chosen. The rest of the day was spent in dancing around the maypole and in feasting.

A-maying during the reign of Queen Elizabeth I

Ascension Day

The fortieth day after Easter is Ascension Day, on which day the resurrected Jesus was seen by the Disciples to 'ascend to Heaven'. This day, like so many Easter festivals, has been celebrated since the fourth century, or even earlier.

In Roman Catholic churches the paschal candle is extinguished. This candle, lit at midnight on Easter Saturday, is a symbol of God's gifts and particularly the gift of the resurrection. So on the day when Jesus left the world, the candle is put out. The word 'paschal' is from the Hebrew word 'pesach' which means 'passover'.

One way of celebrating Ascension Day is 'welldressing'. In the Derbyshire village of Tissington, the five wells are dressed for Ascension Day services. Welldressing is an old and skilful craft. Pictures are worked in flower petals and mosses on a base of clay. The damp clay keeps the pictures fresh for many days, and the village is crowded with visitors who have come to see them.

Whit Sunday

Whitsun is the time of the Jewish feast of Pentecost, when Jews give thanks to God for the harvest. In the second chapter of the Acts of the Apostles, we learn how the Disciples were gathered together for the feast and how they received the gift of the Holy Spirit and became missionaries for Jesus. Pentecost means fiftieth day, for it is the fiftieth day after the Sabbath of the Passover. So it is also fifty days after Easter Sunday.

'Whit Sunday' was once 'White Sunday' because long ago this was the day on which people wore white for their baptism. Baptisms took place at Easter or Pentecost, but in our country Pentecost was more popular as the weather was warmer than at Easter. Perhaps, too, our forefathers remembered how St. Peter baptised on the first Christian Pentecost.

Like Easter, it is a time of enjoyment. In the Middle Ages a special Whitsun ale was brewed and people gathered together to drink it, dance and play games.

Whit walks of Sunday schools and church congregations are a feature of Lancashire towns

October 31st: Halloween

'Hallow' once meant the same as 'saint'. Halloween is short for Allhallows Even, the evening before All Saints' Day. Playing at 'spooks' and witches, games of 'duck apple', eating roast chestnuts, and listening to ghost stories are, however, customs which have their beginnings in remote times.

October 31st was the eve of Samhain, the Druid New Year. It was also the festival of the dead, for the Druids believed that the spirits of the dead visited the living at this time.

When Christianity took the place of this pagan religion, the feast of All Saints took the place of Samhain. However, a few people never became Christian, but continued to believe the Druid ideas. In secret they carried on many of the Druid ceremonies. As time passed some of these ceremonies changed, and the people who took part in them became known as witches, with Samhain their most important feast.

Eating the fruits of autumn, apples and nuts, was part of the Druid feast. When Samhain became Allhallows Even, Christians continued to enjoy these fruits. Games, like 'duck apple' were played around bonfires in which chestnuts were roasted.

In medieval times, bonfires were lit on October 31st as it was thought they frightened off witches

November 5th: Bonfire Night

Remember, remember the fifth of November
Gunpowder treason and plot
I see no reason why gunpowder treason
Should ever be forgot.

Children are not likely to forget Bonfire Night, and while they remember this rhyme they will know the reason for the excitement of bonfires and fireworks.

Once there were wars and serious quarrels over religion. In England everyone was expected to attend the Church of England. Those who did not attend, particularly the Roman Catholics, were forced to pay fines, and often suffered in other ways. When James I became king, he promised to make life easier for these people, but he broke his promise and the persecution became worse. This disappointed the Roman Catholics, and a few fanatics decided to blow up the Houses of Parliament when James was opening the new session on November 5th, 1605.

These conspirators hired a cellar in the Houses of Parliament, and filled it with gunpowder. Some of them warned their friends not to attend the opening of Parliament. The King heard of these warnings and the Houses of Parliament were searched. Guy Fawkes was caught in the cellar, and was later executed with the other conspirators.

The arrest of Guy Fawkes

Remembrance Sunday

The Sunday closest to November 11th is always Remembrance Sunday, on which we remember those who died fighting in two terrible wars of this century. They died that we should be free to rule ourselves.

The First World War ended at 11 a.m. on November 11th, 1918. Soon after, it was decided that the dead should be remembered in two minutes' silence at 11 a.m. every year on this date. Later this was changed to the Sunday nearest this date.

In most towns and villages, war memorials were erected in memory of local men who had died fighting in the war. A large, national memorial, called the Cenotaph, was erected in London, in Whitehall, and every Remembrance Sunday since, at a solemn ceremony, the reigning king or queen has placed on it a wreath of poppies. The men and women who gave their lives fighting in the Second World War are now also remembered at this ceremony.

In the First World War, over five million men of the allied nations died, many of them on the fields of northern France. Although crops were ruined in the fighting, the poppies bloomed, and so the blood-red poppy became the symbol of the tragedy of war. Artificial poppies are sold in the week before Remembrance Sunday, and the money collected is used to help war victims.

November 30th: St. Andrew's Day

St. Andrew's Night is the time of reunion for Scotsmen all over the world. Celebrations may open with the Scottish tradition of piping in the haggis, a meat dish made from the liver, heart, lungs and stomach of an animal.

Like St. George, St. Andrew was not a native of the country whose patron saint he is. He became the patron saint of Scotland after his relics (bones) were brought to the east coast of Scotland, to the town which was later named 'St. Andrews'.

Andrew was a fisherman and a disciple of John the Baptist. John prophesied the coming of Jesus, and Andrew became the first disciple of Jesus. He brought many people to Jesus, the first being his brother Simon Peter. After the Ascension, Andrew is not mentioned in the Bible. He probably preached in the area of the Black Sea, in Greece and Russia. It is likely that he was crucified at Patras, Greece, in 60 A.D. In medieval paintings, he is shown crucified on a diagonal cross. His flag is a white diagonal cross on a blue background. He is also the patron saint of Greece and Russia.

Piping in the haggis

December 25th: Christmas Day

To most boys and girls Christmas Day is the most important day of the year. It is the celebration of the birthday of Christ. 'Christmas' means 'Mass', or church service, for Christ.

Nobody knows at what time of year Jesus was born. Christians who lived a few hundred years after Jesus chose the twenty-fifth of December to remember his birthday, because this was already a special day. Long ago, the twenty-fifth of December was the shortest day of the year and on this day the sun was worshipped. Christians knew that God had made the sun, and so turned the old pagan festival into a day of worship to the 'Son of God'.

Many of the traditions of Christmas have been practised for hundreds and sometimes thousands of years. Decorating our homes with evergreens is a custom much older than the birth of Jesus. So, too, is the giving of gifts at this time of year. Santa Claus, as we know him, and the sending of Christmas cards, are traditions begun less than a hundred years ago.

A model of the Nativity

CONTENTS